VIKING
FACEBOOK ADS

Chapter 1:
Getting Started with Facebook Ads

Despite all the talk you might hear about Facebook ads not working (usually from people who gave up after a couple tries), the fact is that all of the major online entrepreneurs and digital marketers use Facebook ads. Facebook remains the single most attractive advertising opportunity in terms of native ad presentation, targeting, demographic data, active users, and a host of other factors. There are currently almost 1.8 billion monthly active users, almost 1.2 billion daily logins, and 5 new profiles are created every second. With a growing user base like that, it's no wonder more than 40% of marketers report that Facebook is a critical part of their business. The question is, how do you make it work for you?

Establishing Goals

Before you even begin your first ad campaign, you should have your various marketing goals laid out. This will help you determine everything from your campaign objective to your budgeting and bidding. Maybe your goal is to drive cold traffic to a lead page and grow your list. Is that the end of it? In that case you might have a lower spending strategy. But if those leads, after they opt-in to your list, are going to see a tripwire offer and then a core offer and then a profit maximizer (in other words, a full sales funnel), then perhaps you'll be willing to spend more per click. Maybe you're sending them directly to a paid offer or a webinar with a high-ticket offer. Perhaps you're just trying to get visitors to your blog to familiarize them with your brand and provide useful content while also building a retargeting list. Whatever your goals are, have them mapped out before you start creating your ad.

Setting Up Your Page and Ad Account

If you don't already have a "fan page" or business page, you'll need to create one. This is because Facebook advertisements can only be attached to pages, not individual profiles. So take a few moments and set up a page by clicking the "create page" link which can be found at the very bottom of any Facebook page. Choose the category that applies to you (e.g. local business, brand, public figure, etc) and get your bio/about us text and profile and cover images squared away. While you're doing this, you might as well get your page ready for traffic. The thing is, some people who see your ads might not interact specifically the way you want them to. Rather than click through to your site, they often will actually go to your Facebook page and you want to capitalize on that traffic as well. So make sure you at least have a call-to-action (CTA) button at the top of your page that leads somewhere. For now you might as well just choose "sign up" for the CTA and link it to a lead page or landing page of yours. If you don't have a landing page, checkout our Landing Page guide!

Once this is done, simply click the "create ad" button and, if you don't already have an ads account, you'll be prompted to create one. This is a quick process and simply involves some contact info, billing info, and so on. When you're all set, you can move on to creating your first campaign.

Chapter 2: Creating Your Campaign

Upon clicking the "create ad" link or "create campaign" button, you'll be prompted to select an objective. For our purposes we'll say you're aiming for clicks to your website. At the time of this writing, this objective is named "send people to a destination on or off Facebook" but Facebook changes their wording all the time so don't worry if it looks a little different. After choosing your objective you'll need to enter a campaign name and select which of your business/"fan" pages your ad will be attached to.

Audience Targeting

Once you're into the ad set creation page, you'll need to define your audience. This is where the magic starts. Facebook has so much information on their users, it's scary. First, start with the basics. Choose the appropriate target countries, locations, age groups, and genders. Then you can narrow even further by searching for certain job titles, interests, relationship statuses, whether they have children, their spending habits, and so on. For example, if you're targeting business owners to sell email marketing training to, then you could select all ages, both genders, all English-speaking countries, job titles like "small business owner" and "CEO", and interests like "email marketing" and "list building". In fact, with interests you might even try specific autoresponder brand names like GetResponse and Aweber since people who like/follow those companies' pages are likely to be interested in the subject.

Pay close attention to the combination logic you are using. By this I mean "and" vs "or" logic. For example, do you want to choose any people who are interested in **either** Email Marketing "OR" Aweber or do you want to choose only the people who are interested in **both** email marketing AND Aweber? The latter approach is represented by the "narrow audience" button below the targeting box. There may be benefits in some cases to a broad "or logic" approach, but generally you want to get pretty narrow for the most effective targeting.

Be sure to think outside the box too. For example, if you've put together a dog training video course and you want some buyers, most people would just search for "dog training" as an interest. Sure, you could do that and you'd probably have some success. But the real successful marketers think outside the box and target things that only true devotees would be interested in. For example, literally anyone who may have liked a dog training page some time in the past but could care less about the topic might be targeted if you just choose "dog training", but what about a name like "Kyra Sundance"? One of the most popular dog training celebrities in the world? Do you think she might have a Facebook following? Yup. And guess what, if you target people who are interested in her (literally just type her name in the field) you know you're getting hard core dog training enthusiasts, because your average joe who isn't very excited about the topic probably wouldn't be following Kyra Sundance on Facebook!

Take note that as you type words into the interests and other category fields, several related suggestions will pop up below them. Use these suggestions for targeting ideas, but don't worry too much about cramming every possible interest into your targeting. You'll want to write those down on a notepad and save some for later. The reason for this is that in a later chapter we'll be talking about analyzing and optimizing and what you'll be doing is running multiple variations of the same ad with small differences. If you just lump every possible interest into one ad instance, you won't know which interest is most or least effective. We'll save that for chapter 4 but for now just know that there might be a lot of value in having one ad campaign that targets Kyra Sundance as an interest and then another that is exactly the same but it targets Ian Dunbar instead. Then you can shift your dollars towards whichever famous dog trainer performs best as an interest target.

Placements and Pricing

Once you've finalized your targeting, the next step is to decide on placements. Chapter 4 will cover testing different placement types. For now, suffice it to say that you only want one placement per ad so you can later compare and determine which placement works best for you. For our purposes let's choose desktop newsfeeds for this one.

After that, it's time to think about your budget. Since we're just starting out and we don't know what's effective, it's best to start small. Let's try a $5 daily budget and let it run for 5 days. Although it's fine to experiment with various optimization options later on, for now you just want to pay for your actual results, so under "optimize for", choose "clicks to website/pay per click" not "impressions". When it comes to bidding, you want to choose manual and ensure you're inside the recommended bid range, but there's no need to be high within that range. Unless you have some sort of deadline there's no need to pay more to get faster results. So aim for something in the lower half of the recommended range (e.g. $1.12 if the recommended range is $0.92 to $2.14). You can always adjust these later.

When you're satisfied, click "continue" and let's start developing your ad creative!

Chapter 3:
The Creative

Ad Format

When setting up your ad creative, you'll see multiple format options including single image, single video, carousel, canvas (new) and slideshow. Single image simply means one image will be displayed, but you can add up to 6 images and Facebook will cycle which one displays for each impression. Single video is self-explanatory, and slideshow means Facebook will create a looping video with up to 10 images. Carousel means the ad will rotate through multiple images while it's being viewed by one person. Canvas is a new addition which incorporates images and videos. Same story: Focus on the single image option this time and experiment with the others later.

Image Design

For the image design, you want to aim for 1200 x 628 pixels in size but this can vary depending on ad format and keep in mind Facebook might change this in the future, so always look at the recommended size. Be sure to use high quality images. These can be stock images, funny images, even just a portrait of you if you're pitching a personal brand.

There are two things to keep in mind when using images. First, you want to minimize text on the image. People often think they'd like to cram their textual message into the image itself so it's not missed, but Facebook has determined this is actually less effective and that it annoys users. If your text takes up more than about 20% of your image's area, then you risk your ad being shown less or not at all.

Second, you want to think about "ad scent". It's been proven that conversions are much better if the destination page has the same look and feel as the ad they clicked on to get there. This doesn't mean it needs to be exactly the same, but take basic factors into consideration like brightness/darkness and primary colors and anything else that might help your landing page look and feel similar to the ad image. For example, if you're using a stock image of a business woman in the ad, consider either the same image or an image with the same model on the landing page.

Ad Copy

Lastly, you'll have to draft your ad headline, ad body text, and link description text. Make sure your text clearly conveys what you're offering. There is no one rule on whether your ad copy should be short or long so you'll have to experiment a bit in the future to see what your audience likes best. You can also add a prettier version of your website URL to be displayed. Finally, you'll have the option of choosing a CTA button such as "learn more" or "book now". Once finished, click "place order" and get ready to start analyzing your results!

Chapter 4: Analyze and Optimize

The number one reason people give up on Facebook ads is because their first experience is underwhelming. This is a big mistake. Facebook advertising works. The trick is to test, analyze, and optimize. Here's how you do that.

Multiple Variations

If you'll recall from previous chapters, we discussed that you might want to experiment with various different settings. Problem is, if you cram all these experimental factors into one ad, you won't know what worked and what drags your effectiveness down. Remember, you're spending money on these clicks. It's important to know what the effects are of all these variables so you can get the best bang for your buck. The way to do this is simply to do a separate ad for each different factor you are testing.

There are several things to test. As we mentioned earlier, you could run one ad set targeting one interest and have another identical ad set with a different interest. For example, perhaps people who are interested in GetResponse are more enthusiastic about email marketing-related ads and more likely to click or signup than people interested in Aweber. Perhaps placements on mobile newsfeeds work better than Instagram. Maybe one headline gets more clicks than another. Maybe the photo of you in front of your desk beats the stock image of the business man in the white shirt. All of these could have an impact on your results and costs. The key is to make sure that each time you compare, you're only looking at one change. If you change more than one thing at a time, then you might see an improvement, but you'll never know if it was caused by the gal in the red dress or the more wordy headline. Moreover, your results could theoretically have been better but you'd never discover that. For example, what if the wordy headline did result in 6 additional clicks per 1,000 impressions, but the gal in the red dress was costing an average decrease of 2 clicks? Knowing this would mean you could actually enjoy an additional 8 clicks per 1,000 impressions, but since you didn't know that you'll never get those extra clicks and the red dress gal will keep dragging you down slightly throughout your future campaigns. One final thought on conversion testing is that you might consider sending people to a different variation of your landing page for each ad, too, in order to see which ad works best with which landing page (remember what we said about ad scent?). It's just another opportunity to squeeze more results out of each dollar you spend and it can be quite easy if you use a landing page creator like Instapage. Check out our guides on split testing and landing page creation to learn more about all this.

Once we've created all these tests and comparisons, the next step is simple. Analyze the results and then discontinue the losers and put more dollars into the winners. You can do this easily by pausing or stopping the variations that don't work as well and by editing any of your campaigns and increasing the budget or scheduled ad run time. Then, start testing other variations. Tweak this, then that, keep it to one change at a time and adjust accordingly. Bottom line, if you test thoroughly and carefully, you WILL maximize your results per dollar spent.

Battle Plan

Facebook can be an excellent resource for your business. The key to avoiding the fate of so many naysayers is to start small, test different variations, adjust accordingly, and scale upwards. This guide has given you an excellent path forward, but it won't mean anything if you set down this book and don't implement what you learned. Start applying the steps of this battle plan today:

Step 1: Determine your goals ahead of time.

Step 2: Set up your business page and ad account if you haven't already.

Step 3: Create your campaign and ad set with specific targeting.

Step 4: Create your ad image and text.

Step 5: Clone the ad set and experiment with a few variations of format, image, copy, and targeting.

Step 6: Analyze your results and optimize accordingly.

www.ingramcontent.com/pod-product-compliance
Lightning Source LLC
Chambersburg PA
CBRC090852210326
41597CB00011B/176